Somebody Catch
My Homework

Somebody Catch

Poems b

Illustrated b

My Homework

David L. Harrison
Betsy Lewin

SCHOLASTIC INC.

New York Toronto London Auckland Sydney
Mexico City New Delhi Hong Kong Buenos Aires

For our Robin
and her Tim
and their Kristopher.
D.H.

To Leonard Grade,
where I went to school
with kids just like the ones
in all of these poems.
B.L.

ISBN 0-439-69100-1

Text copyright © 1993 by David L. Harrison.
Illustrations copyright © 1993 by Betsy Lewin.
All rights reserved. Published by Scholastic Inc.,
557 Broadway, New York, NY 10012, by arrangement
with Boyds Mills Press. SCHOLASTIC and associated logos
are trademarks and/or registered trademarks of Scholastic Inc.

12 11 10 9 8 7 6 5 4 3 2 1   4 5 6 7 8 9/0

Printed in the U.S.A.   40

First Scholastic printing, September 2004

Book designed by Charlotte Staub
The text of this book is set in 14-point Clarendon.
The illustrations are done in watercolors.

CONTENTS

TEN MINUTES TILL THE BUS

Ten whole minutes
Till the bus,
Scads of time,
What's the fuss?
Two to dress,
One to flush,
Two to eat,
One to brush,
That leaves four
To catch the bus,
Scads of time,
What's the fuss?

MONDAY!

Overslept
Rain is pouring
Missed the bus
Dad is roaring
Late for school
Forgot my spelling
Soaking wet
Clothes are smelling
Dropped my books
Got them muddy
Flunked a test
Didn't study
Teacher says
I must do better
Lost my money
Tore my sweater
Feeling dumber
Feeling glummer
Monday sure can be
A bummer.

SHOW AND TELL

Billy brought his snake to school
For show and tell today.
"This snake belongs to me," he said.
"It's gentle as can be," he said.
"It wouldn't hurt a flea," he said.
But it swallowed him anyway.

MY EXCUSE

But I did do my homework!
Yes ma'am!
I really really did!
Un-huh.
Mama wrapped fish bones in it.
See?
She really really did!
Un-huh.
And them old fish bones
Stinked up the kitchen
Till Daddy throwed 'em out.
Un-huh!
Now our neighbor, she's old,
And she's got an old cat,
And she got in our trash can.
See?

And she run down the street
With my homework!
No ma'am,
The old cat, not the old lady.
Now the old man on the other side,
He's got an old dog,
And he run after that cat
Yellin' awful!
No ma'am,
The old man, not the old dog.
He's too old!
Yes ma'am.
So I looked out the window
And let out a yell
And hightailed it
After the old man.
See?
"Somebody catch my homework!"
I yelled.
Yes ma'am.
Loud as I could!

So my brother run past me
And past the old man
And he grabbed them fish bones
From that old cat
And he run home grinnin'!
But we all held our noses
'Cause it smelled bad!
His hand, not my homework.
So Daddy he took
And buried it in the yard.
No ma'am,
My homework, not brother's hand.
And I couldn't do nothin' about it.
So see?
And by then it was late.
Really really late!
There wasn't nothin' I could do!
And that's purely the truth!
Believe me?
Yes ma'am!
Un-huh!

A BETTER ANSWER

Bradley always answers!
We hate it when he answers!
His hand is always shooting up
To make us all look bad.
Teacher says to study.
Study! Study! Study!
But studying's not the answer—
It's getting rid of Brad!

RALPHY

Ralphy drawed a caterpillar,
Boy did teacher squawk!
Ralphy drawed it twelve feet long
And drawed up all the chalk.

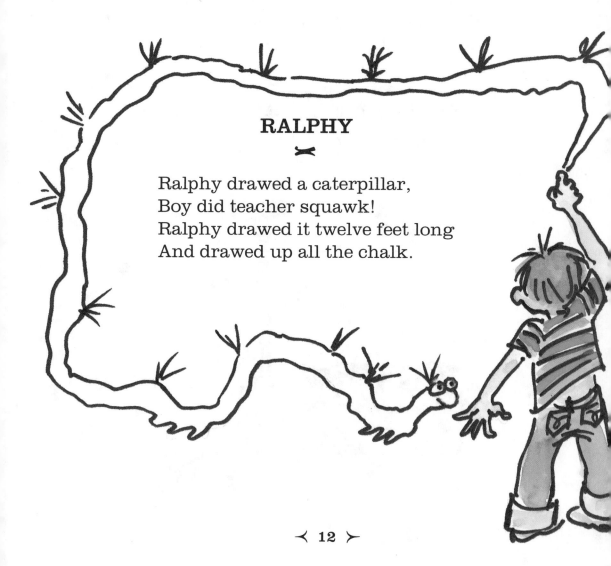

MY ADVICE

Elizabeth Ann and Betty Lou Morse
Said, "We're so hungry
We could eat a horse!"
So my advice, if you're a horse, is
Whatever you do,
Avoid the Morses.

WHATEVER

I ruined my pants
When I slud in the mud.
Teacher says,
"It's slid, not slud."
Now I don't care
If it's slud or slid,
I ruined my pants
When I slid in the mid.

ONE THING ON MY MIND

✂

I've gottogotothebathroom
The bathroom the bathroom
I've gottogotothebathroom
Is all that I can say.
If Idon'tgettthererightaway
Right away right away
If Idon'tgettthererightaway
It will ruin the rest of my day.

CURSIVE WRITING

Who decides?
Who gets to choose?
Who dreams up these curlicues?
Should an *%* look like
A 9 and a 6?
Fiddlesticks!
Does a capital q
That looks like a 2
Make sense to you?
Do I like these
Wiggles
And squiggles
And jiggles?
Hah!
What do I think
of cursive writing?
Bah!

BOBBY GENE McQUIG

The worst boy in the whole class
Is Bobby Gene McQuig.
He's wilder than a billygoat
And meaner than a pig.
His shirttail's always hanging out,
His upper lip is green,
And if you like to cheat and fight,
You'd love old Bobby Gene.

Every kid in the whole class
Would like to see him dead,
But we're afraid that he will be
The death of us instead.
This morning he was showing off
In front of Chris and Rose
And just to make them sick he stuck
His finger up his nose.

Miss Wilson grabbed for Bobby Gene
So fast he couldn't duck.
"You take that finger out!" she cried.
"I can't!" he said. "It's stuck!"
We laughed so hard at Bobby Gene
That he began to shout, "It won't be quite so funny
When I get my finger out!"

Miss Wilson couldn't pry it loose
And neither could the nurse.
She sent for Dr. Applegate
Who only made things worse.
"I've never seen a stranger case,"
Said Dr. Applegate.
"Because your finger's stuck so tight
I cannot operate.
I cannot move it up or down
And therefore I suppose
You'll simply have to learn to live
With your finger up your nose.
I'm going to give you aspirin
And send you home to bed."
"I've got some things I gotta do,"
Was all that Bobby said.

He swaggered back to class at noon
And belched and spit on Matt.
He shoved Lavern against the wall
And wiped his hand on Pat.
He got right up in Chris's face
And stomped on Bubba's toes.
He's the worst boy in the whole world
With his finger up his nose!

NEW HERE?

You'll love the food at our school,
Oh yes!
The lumps in the potatoes are glue
We guess.
The beef never mooed like a cow
You can bet
Though very few kids have died from it . . .
Yet.
The rolls are great to stone squirrels
From trees
But some of us blast them with
Buckshot peas.
The applesauce is a watery
Goo
But suck it right down 'cause it's good
For you.
The best, of course, we all save
For last—
Bouncing our Jell-O down the hall
Real fast.

LAST NIGHT

Last night I knew the answers.
Last night I had them pat.
Last night I could have told you
Every answer, just like that!
Last night my brain was cooking.
Last night I got them right.
Last night I was a genius.
So where were you last night!

THE TEST

It's not my fault if I flunked the test.
This room's too cold to do my best.
My foot's asleep,
I lost my gum,
I've got a fever,
This pencil's dumb,
My collar's tight,
There's a pain in my head,
I couldn't hear
A thing you said,
My throat is sore,
I need a drink,
Billy's humming,
I can't think,
And . . .
What's that? You say I passed the test?
Well, if I do say so, I did my best.

LOVE

I love Johnny
But he loves Sue
And she loves Bill
Who's crazy for Lu
Who's wild for Paul
Who's in love with Fay.
Now Fay loves Pete
But Pete loves Kay
And she loves Tim
Who thinks I'm neat.
I tell you love
Is hard to beat.

WHY THE PRESIDENT IS THE PRESIDENT

Tim chewed gum, poor guy,
Now why would he try that?
Dick, the rat, told Mrs. Cook
Who shook her finger at Tim
And yelled at him,
"Spit out that gum!"

"That's dumb," said he,
"It's a fresh stick, see?
But I'll chew it quick."
But thanks to Dick,
He was soon in the principal's office.

The principal got furious
And Tim, acting curious, asked,
"What's so bad that you're so mad
Over one stick of gum?"

"Well!" the principal yelled,
"You must be slow not to know
That chewing gum in class is crass
And schools have rules
Against that sort of thing.
So spit out that gum, you bum,
And apologize!"

But Tim unwisely giggled instead.
The principal turned red
And called out the National Guard
With planes and tanks
And several ranks of officers
Who scowled at him and bellowed,
"Tim! Take out that gum!
"It's wrong to be doing it!"

But Tim kept chewing it
Until somebody sent for the Governor
Who flew in right away that day
Just to say, "You spit out that gum!"
But Tim said, "How come?"
So the Governor fired a wire
To the President and turned Tim in
For breaking school rules
And the President came and said,
"Be a good kid, Tim,
"Please spit out your gum,"
And Tim did.

So everybody clapped and asked,
"How come you finally decided
To spit out your gum?"
And Tim explained it with ease.
"The President," he said,
"Said please."

I'D RATHER NOT

To you it's only homework,
But I'm half wild with fright!
You said to write two pages
And get them done tonight!

Give me a thousand problems,
I'll work until they're right,
But Teacher, Teacher PLEASE don't make me
Write two pages tonight!

I'm really good at reading,
At spelling you've said I'm bright,
But the thought of two whole pages
Is turning my hair all white.

Test me till I'm dizzy,
I'll try with all my might,
Give me a break,
I'm nearly in tears,
I'll praise your name,
I'll shout three cheers,
I'll study hard
For a hundred years,
Scold me,
Whip me,
Pull my ears!
Only DON'T make me write
TONIGHT!

NEVER AGAIN!

What's tougher than crossing the desert
On your knees?
What's harder than hopping up a mountain
On the double?
What's worse than sitting in a cave
Till you freeze?
Walking to the principal's office . . .
In trouble.

NOT FAIR

Sitting in school
On an April day
Isn't fair.
A guy should be flying
A kite with the wind
In his hair.
I know I'm supposed
To be doing my math,
I don't care.
Sitting in school
On an April day
Isn't fair.

MY BOOK!

I did it!
I did it!
Come and look
At what I've done!
I read a book!
When someone wrote it
Long ago
For me to read,
How did he know
That this was the book
I'd take from the shelf
And lie on the floor
And read by myself?
I really read it!
Just like that!
Word by word,
From first to last!
I'm sleeping with
This book in bed,
This first FIRST book
I've ever read!